Gazpacho Cookbook

By Brad Hoskinson

Table of Contents

Classic Spanish Gazpacho:

Classic Spanish Gazpacho is a refreshing and savory cold soup perfect for hot summer days. It blends fresh vegetables and herbs, creating a delightful and healthy dish.

Prep Time: 15 minutes

Ingredients:

- ✓ 6 ripe tomatoes, chopped
- ✓ 1 cucumber, peeled and chopped
- ✓ 1 red bell pepper, chopped
- ✓ 1 small red onion, chopped
- ✓ 2 cloves garlic, minced
- ✓ 3 cups tomato juice
- ✓ 1/4 cup red wine vinegar
- ✓ 1/4 cup extra-virgin olive oil
- ✓ 1 teaspoon salt
- ✓ 1/2 teaspoon black pepper
- ✓ 1/2 teaspoon sugar (optional)
- ✓ Croutons, for garnish (optional)

Method:

1. Combine the chopped tomatoes, cucumber, red bell pepper, red onion, and minced garlic in a blender or food processor. Pulse until the mixture is finely chopped but not completely smooth.
2. Transfer the mixture to a large bowl, and then add the tomato juice, red wine vinegar, olive oil, salt, black pepper, and sugar (if using). Mix well to combine.

3. Cover the bowl and refrigerate the gazpacho for at least 2 hours, allowing the flavors to meld and the soup to chill.
4. Before serving, taste and adjust the seasonings if needed. Add more salt, pepper, or vinegar to suit your taste.
5. Serve the Classic Spanish Gazpacho cold, garnished with croutons if desired.

Watermelon Mint Gazpacho:

Watermelon Mint Gazpacho is a delightful twist on the classic recipe, adding watermelon's sweet and refreshing flavor and the aromatic touch of mint.

Prep Time: 15 minutes

Ingredients:

- ✓ 4 cups diced seedless watermelon
- ✓ 1 cucumber, peeled and chopped
- ✓ 1/4 cup fresh mint leaves
- ✓ 2 tablespoons lime juice
- ✓ 1/4 teaspoon salt
- ✓ 1/4 teaspoon black pepper
- ✓ 1/4 teaspoon cayenne pepper (optional)
- ✓ 1/4 cup crumbled feta cheese (optional)
- ✓ Fresh mint leaves for garnish

Method:

1. In a blender or food processor, Combine the diced watermelon, cucumber, fresh mint leaves, lime juice, salt, black pepper, and cayenne pepper (if using). Blend until smooth.
2. Taste the gazpacho and adjust the seasoning if needed by adding more salt or lime juice.
3. Chill the Watermelon Mint Gazpacho in the refrigerator for at least 30 minutes before serving.
4. If desired, Serve the gazpacho cold, garnished with crumbled feta cheese and fresh mint leaves.

Andalusian Tomato Gazpacho:

Andalusian Tomato Gazpacho is a traditional Spanish recipe hailing from the Andalusian region. It's known for its simple, fresh, and vibrant flavors.

Prep Time: 15 minutes

Ingredients:

- ✓ 6 ripe tomatoes, peeled and chopped
- ✓ 1 cucumber, peeled and chopped
- ✓ 1 red bell pepper, chopped
- ✓ 1 small red onion, chopped
- ✓ 2 cloves garlic, minced
- ✓ 3 cups tomato juice
- ✓ 1/4 cup red wine vinegar
- ✓ 1/4 cup extra-virgin olive oil
- ✓ 1 teaspoon salt
- ✓ 1/2 teaspoon black pepper
- ✓ 1/2 teaspoon smoked paprika
- ✓ Croutons and chopped fresh parsley for garnish (optional)

Method:

1. Combine the peeled and chopped tomatoes, cucumber, red bell pepper, red onion, and minced garlic in a blender or food processor. Blend until smooth.
2. Pour the tomato mixture into a large bowl. Add the tomato juice, red wine vinegar, olive oil, salt, black pepper, and smoked paprika. Stir well to combine.

3. Chill the Andalusian Tomato Gazpacho in the refrigerator for at least 2 hours before serving.
4. Serve the gazpacho cold, garnished with croutons and chopped fresh parsley if desired.

Cucumber Avocado Gazpacho:

Cucumber Avocado Gazpacho is a creamy and refreshing variation of the traditional gazpacho, enriched with the smoothness of ripe avocados.

Prep Time: 15 minutes

Ingredients:

- ✓ 2 cucumbers, peeled and chopped
- ✓ 2 ripe avocados, peeled and pitted
- ✓ 1/4 cup fresh cilantro leaves
- ✓ 2 cloves garlic, minced
- ✓ 3 cups vegetable broth
- ✓ 2 tablespoons lime juice
- ✓ 1/2 teaspoon cumin
- ✓ Salt and black pepper to taste
- ✓ Sliced cucumber and cilantro leaves for garnish

Method:

1. Combine the chopped cucumbers, ripe avocados, fresh cilantro leaves, minced garlic, vegetable broth, lime juice, and cumin in a blender or food processor. Blend until the mixture is smooth and creamy.
2. Season the Cucumber Avocado Gazpacho with salt and black pepper to taste. Adjust the seasoning if needed.
3. Chill the gazpacho in the refrigerator for at least 30 minutes before serving.
4. Serve the gazpacho cold, garnished with sliced cucumber and fresh cilantro leaves.

Roasted Red Pepper Gazpacho:

Roasted Red Pepper Gazpacho is a smoky and slightly sweet variation of gazpacho, thanks to the roasted red peppers.

Prep Time: 15 minutes

Ingredients:

- ✓ 3 red bell peppers, roasted, peeled, and chopped
- ✓ 3 ripe tomatoes, chopped
- ✓ 1 cucumber, peeled and chopped
- ✓ 1/4 cup red onion, chopped
- ✓ 2 cloves garlic, minced
- ✓ 3 cups tomato juice
- ✓ 2 tablespoons red wine vinegar
- ✓ 2 tablespoons extra-virgin olive oil
- ✓ 1 teaspoon smoked paprika
- ✓ Salt and black pepper to taste
- ✓ Fresh basil leaves for garnish

Method:

1. Begin by roasting the red bell peppers. Place them on a baking sheet and broil in the oven, turning occasionally, until the skins are charred and blistered. Remove from the oven, let cool, peel, remove seeds, and chop.
2. Combine the roasted red peppers, chopped tomatoes, cucumber, red onion, minced garlic, tomato juice, red wine vinegar, extra-virgin olive oil, and smoked paprika in a blender or food processor. Blend until smooth.

3. Season the Roasted Red Pepper Gazpacho with salt and black pepper to taste. Adjust the seasoning if needed.
4. Chill the gazpacho in the refrigerator for at least 2 hours before serving.
5. Serve the gazpacho cold, garnished with fresh basil leaves.

Strawberry Basil Gazpacho:

Strawberry Basil Gazpacho is a delightful twist on traditional gazpacho, featuring strawberries' sweet and fruity flavors complemented by fresh basil's aromatic touch.

Prep Time: 15 minutes

Ingredients:

- ✓ 2 cups ripe strawberries, hulled and halved
- ✓ 1 cucumber, peeled and chopped
- ✓ 1 small red bell pepper, chopped
- ✓ 1/4 cup red onion, chopped
- ✓ 2 cloves garlic, minced
- ✓ 2 tablespoons balsamic vinegar
- ✓ 1/4 cup fresh basil leaves
- ✓ 1/4 cup tomato juice
- ✓ 1/4 cup water
- ✓ Salt and black pepper to taste
- ✓ Fresh strawberry slices and basil leaves for garnish

Method:

1. Combine the ripe strawberries, cucumber, red bell pepper, red onion, minced garlic, balsamic vinegar, fresh basil leaves, tomato juice, and water in a blender or food processor. Blend until smooth.
2. Season the Strawberry Basil Gazpacho with salt and black pepper to taste. Adjust the seasoning if needed.
3. Chill the gazpacho in the refrigerator for at least 30 minutes before serving.

4. Serve the gazpacho cold, garnished with fresh strawberry slices and basil leaves.

Green Gazpacho with Herbs:

Introduction: Green Gazpacho with Herbs is a vibrant and herbaceous variation of gazpacho featuring a medley of fresh green vegetables and aromatic herbs.

Prep Time: 20 minutes

Ingredients:

- ✓ 2 cups chopped cucumber
- ✓ 1 cup chopped green bell pepper
- ✓ 1 cup chopped celery
- ✓ 1/2 cup chopped green onion
- ✓ 1/4 cup fresh cilantro leaves
- ✓ 1/4 cup fresh parsley leaves
- ✓ 2 cloves garlic, minced
- ✓ 3 cups vegetable broth
- ✓ 2 tablespoons white wine vinegar
- ✓ 2 tablespoons extra-virgin olive oil
- ✓ Salt and black pepper to taste
- ✓ Sliced green onions and fresh herbs for garnish

Method:

1. In a blender or food processor, Combine the chopped cucumber, green bell pepper, celery, green onion, cilantro leaves, parsley leaves, minced garlic, vegetable broth, white wine vinegar, and extra-virgin olive oil. Blend until smooth.
2. Season the Green Gazpacho with Herbs with salt and black pepper to taste. Adjust the seasoning if needed.

3. Chill the gazpacho in the refrigerator for at least 30 minutes before serving.
4. Serve the gazpacho cold, garnished with sliced green onions and fresh herbs.

White Grape Gazpacho:

White Grape Gazpacho is a unique and refreshing variation that combines the sweetness of white grapes with the savory elements of gazpacho.

Prep Time: 15 minutes

Ingredients:

- ✓ 2 cups seedless white grapes
- ✓ 1 cucumber, peeled and chopped
- ✓ 1/4 cup blanched almonds
- ✓ 1/4 cup fresh mint leaves
- ✓ 2 cloves garlic, minced
- ✓ 2 cups vegetable broth
- ✓ 2 tablespoons white wine vinegar
- ✓ 2 tablespoons extra-virgin olive oil
- ✓ Salt and white pepper to taste
- ✓ Fresh mint leaves and sliced grapes for garnish

Method:

1. Combine the seedless white grapes, cucumber, blanched almonds, fresh mint leaves, minced garlic, vegetable broth, white wine vinegar, and extra-virgin olive oil in a blender or food processor. Blend until smooth.
2. Season the White Grape Gazpacho with salt and white pepper to taste. Adjust the seasoning if needed.
3. Chill the gazpacho in the refrigerator for at least 30 minutes before serving.

4. Serve the gazpacho cold, garnished with fresh mint leaves and sliced grapes.

Mango Pineapple Gazpacho:

Mango Pineapple Gazpacho is a tropical and fruity take on gazpacho, featuring the sweetness of mango and pineapple.

Prep Time: 15 minutes

Ingredients:

- ✓ 2 ripe mangoes, peeled and chopped
- ✓ 1 cup fresh pineapple chunks
- ✓ 1 cucumber, peeled and chopped
- ✓ 1/4 cup red onion, chopped
- ✓ 2 cloves garlic, minced
- ✓ 1/4 cup fresh cilantro leaves
- ✓ 2 tablespoons lime juice
- ✓ 2 cups vegetable broth
- ✓ Salt and black pepper to taste
- ✓ Fresh cilantro and diced mango for garnish

1. ## Method:

2. Combine the chopped mangoes, fresh pineapple chunks, cucumber, red onion, minced garlic, fresh cilantro leaves, lime juice, and vegetable broth in a blender or food processor. Blend until smooth.
3. Season the Mango Pineapple Gazpacho with salt and black pepper to taste. Adjust the seasoning if needed.
4. Chill the gazpacho in the refrigerator for at least 30 minutes before serving.
5. Serve the gazpacho cold, garnished with fresh cilantro and diced mango.

Spicy Jalapeño Gazpacho:

Spicy Jalapeño Gazpacho adds a kick of heat to the traditional gazpacho recipe, making it perfect for those who enjoy a bit of spice.

Prep Time: 15 minutes

Ingredients:

- ✓ 6 ripe tomatoes, chopped
- ✓ 1 cucumber, peeled and chopped
- ✓ 1 red bell pepper, chopped
- ✓ 2 jalapeño peppers, seeded and chopped
- ✓ 1 small red onion, chopped
- ✓ 2 cloves garlic, minced
- ✓ 3 cups tomato juice
- ✓ 1/4 cup red wine vinegar
- ✓ 1/4 cup extra-virgin olive oil
- ✓ 1 teaspoon salt
- ✓ 1/2 teaspoon black pepper
- ✓ 1/2 teaspoon cayenne pepper (adjust to taste)
- ✓ Sliced jalapeños and cilantro leaves for garnish

Method:

1. Combine the chopped tomatoes, cucumber, red bell pepper, jalapeño peppers, red onion, and minced garlic in a blender or food processor. Blend until finely chopped but not completely smooth.

2. Transfer the mixture to a large bowl and add the tomato juice, red wine vinegar, olive oil, salt, black pepper, and cayenne pepper. Mix well to combine.
3. Chill the Spicy Jalapeño Gazpacho in the refrigerator for at least 2 hours before serving.
4. Serve the gazpacho cold, garnished with sliced jalapeños and cilantro leaves.

Greek Tzatziki Gazpacho:

Greek Tzatziki Gazpacho combines the flavors of traditional Greek tzatziki sauce with the refreshing elements of gazpacho, creating a delightful fusion of Mediterranean flavors.

Prep Time: 15 minutes

Ingredients:

- ✓ 2 cups Greek yogurt
- ✓ 1 cucumber, peeled, seeded, and grated
- ✓ 2 cloves garlic, minced
- ✓ 2 tablespoons fresh dill, chopped
- ✓ 2 tablespoons fresh mint, chopped
- ✓ 1 tablespoon lemon juice
- ✓ 2 cups vegetable broth
- ✓ Salt and black pepper to taste
- ✓ Chopped cucumber, dill, and mint for garnish

Method:

1. Combine the Greek yogurt, grated cucumber, minced garlic, chopped dill, chopped mint, and lemon juice in a large bowl. Mix until well combined.
2. Gradually whisk the vegetable broth until the mixture reaches your desired soup consistency.
3. Season the Greek Tzatziki Gazpacho with salt and black pepper to taste. Adjust the seasoning if needed.
4. Chill the gazpacho in the refrigerator for at least 30 minutes before serving.

5. Serve the gazpacho cold, garnished with chopped cucumber, dill, and mint.

Corn and Red Onion Gazpacho:

Corn and Red Onion Gazpacho is a sweet and savory variation of gazpacho featuring the flavors of fresh corn and red onions.

Prep Time: 15 minutes

Ingredients:

- ✓ 2 cups fresh corn kernels (from about 4 ears of corn)
- ✓ 1 red onion, chopped
- ✓ 1 red bell pepper, chopped
- ✓ 2 cloves garlic, minced
- ✓ 3 cups vegetable broth
- ✓ 1/4 cup red wine vinegar
- ✓ 1/4 cup extra-virgin olive oil
- ✓ Salt and black pepper to taste
- ✓ Fresh cilantro leaves and chopped red onion for garnish

Method:

1. Combine the fresh corn kernels, chopped red onion, red bell pepper, minced garlic, vegetable broth, red wine vinegar, and extra-virgin olive oil in a blender or food processor. Blend until smooth.
2. Season the Corn and Red Onion Gazpacho with salt and black pepper to taste. Adjust the seasoning if needed.
3. Chill the gazpacho in the refrigerator for at least 30 minutes before serving.
4. Serve the gazpacho cold, garnished with fresh cilantro leaves and chopped red onion.

Smoky Chipotle Gazpacho:

Smoky Chipotle Gazpacho adds a smoky and spicy twist to the classic gazpacho, thanks to the addition of chipotle peppers in adobo sauce.

Prep Time: 15 minutes

Ingredients:

- ✓ 6 ripe tomatoes, chopped
- ✓ 1 cucumber, peeled and chopped
- ✓ 1 red bell pepper, chopped
- ✓ 1 small red onion, chopped
- ✓ 2 cloves garlic, minced
- ✓ 2 chipotle peppers in adobo sauce (adjust to taste)
- ✓ 3 cups tomato juice
- ✓ 1/4 cup red wine vinegar
- ✓ 1/4 cup extra-virgin olive oil
- ✓ Salt and black pepper to taste
- ✓ Fresh cilantro leaves and sour cream for garnish

Method:

1. Combine the chopped tomatoes, cucumber, red bell pepper, red onion, minced garlic, chipotle peppers in adobo sauce, tomato juice, red wine vinegar, and extra-virgin olive oil in a blender or food processor. Blend until smooth.
2. Season the Smoky Chipotle Gazpacho with salt and black pepper to taste. Adjust the seasoning if needed.

3. Chill the gazpacho in the refrigerator for at least 2 hours before serving.
4. If desired, serve the gazpacho cold, garnished with fresh cilantro leaves and a dollop of sour cream.

Beet and Fennel Gazpacho:

Beet and Fennel Gazpacho is a vibrant and earthy variation of gazpacho, featuring the sweetness of beets and the subtle licorice notes of fennel.

Prep Time: 15 minutes

Ingredients:

- ✓ 2 large beets, roasted, peeled, and chopped
- ✓ 1 fennel bulb, chopped
- ✓ 1 cucumber, peeled and chopped
- ✓ 2 cloves garlic, minced
- ✓ 3 cups vegetable broth
- ✓ 2 tablespoons red wine vinegar
- ✓ 2 tablespoons extra-virgin olive oil
- ✓ Salt and black pepper to taste
- ✓ Fresh fennel fronds and beet slices for garnish

Method:

1. Combine the roasted and chopped beets, fennel bulb, cucumber, minced garlic, vegetable broth, red wine vinegar, and extra-virgin olive oil in a blender or food processor. Blend until smooth.
2. Season the Beet and Fennel Gazpacho with salt and black pepper to taste. Adjust the seasoning if needed.
3. Chill the gazpacho in the refrigerator for at least 30 minutes before serving.
4. Serve the gazpacho cold, garnished with fresh fennel fronds and beet slices.

Carrot Ginger Gazpacho:

Carrot Ginger Gazpacho is a vibrant and slightly spicy variation of gazpacho featuring the sweetness of carrots and the warmth of ginger.

Prep Time: 15 minutes

Ingredients:

- ✓ 2 cups carrots, peeled and chopped
- ✓ 1 cucumber, peeled and chopped
- ✓ 1 small red onion, chopped
- ✓ 2 cloves garlic, minced
- ✓ 2 tablespoons fresh ginger, minced
- ✓ 3 cups vegetable broth
- ✓ 2 tablespoons rice vinegar
- ✓ 2 tablespoons sesame oil
- ✓ Salt and black pepper to taste
- ✓ Fresh cilantro leaves and sesame seeds for garnish

Method:

1. Combine the chopped carrots, cucumber, red onion, minced garlic, ginger, vegetable broth, rice vinegar, and sesame oil in a blender or food processor. Blend until smooth.
2. Season the Carrot Ginger Gazpacho with salt and black pepper to taste. Adjust the seasoning if needed.
3. Chill the gazpacho in the refrigerator for at least 30 minutes before serving.

4. Serve the gazpacho cold, garnished with fresh cilantro leaves and sesame seeds.

Blueberry Balsamic Gazpacho:

Blueberry Balsamic Gazpacho is a unique and sweet variation of gazpacho, featuring the vibrant flavors of blueberries and the tangy kick of balsamic vinegar.

Prep Time: 15 minutes

Ingredients:

- ✓ 2 cups fresh blueberries
- ✓ 1 cucumber, peeled and chopped
- ✓ 1 small red onion, chopped
- ✓ 2 cloves garlic, minced
- ✓ 3 cups vegetable broth
- ✓ 1/4 cup balsamic vinegar
- ✓ 1/4 cup extra-virgin olive oil
- ✓ Salt and black pepper to taste
- ✓ Fresh blueberries and mint leaves for garnish

Method:

1. Combine the fresh blueberries, chopped cucumber, red onion, minced garlic, vegetable broth, balsamic vinegar, and extra-virgin olive oil in a blender or food processor. Blend until smooth.
2. Season the Blueberry Balsamic Gazpacho with salt and black pepper to taste. Adjust the seasoning if needed.
3. Chill the gazpacho in the refrigerator for at least 30 minutes before serving.
4. Serve the gazpacho cold, garnished with fresh blueberries and mint leaves.

Spinach and Cilantro Gazpacho:

Spinach and Cilantro Gazpacho is a vibrant green variation of gazpacho, featuring the freshness of spinach and the bright flavor of cilantro.

Prep Time: 15 minutes

Ingredients:

- ✓ 2 cups fresh spinach leaves
- ✓ 1 cup fresh cilantro leaves
- ✓ 1 cucumber, peeled and chopped
- ✓ 1 green bell pepper, chopped
- ✓ 1 small red onion, chopped
- ✓ 2 cloves garlic, minced
- ✓ 3 cups vegetable broth
- ✓ 2 tablespoons lime juice
- ✓ 2 tablespoons extra-virgin olive oil
- ✓ Salt and black pepper to taste
- ✓ Fresh cilantro leaves and sliced green onions for garnish

Method:

1. Combine the fresh spinach, cilantro, chopped cucumber, green bell pepper, red onion, minced garlic, vegetable broth, lime juice, and extra-virgin olive oil in a blender or food processor. Blend until smooth.
2. Season the Spinach and Cilantro Gazpacho with salt and black pepper to taste. Adjust the seasoning if needed.
3. Chill the gazpacho in the refrigerator for at least 30 minutes before serving.

4. Serve the gazpacho cold, garnished with fresh cilantro leaves and sliced green onions.

Lemon Cucumber Gazpacho:

Lemon Cucumber Gazpacho is a zesty and refreshing variation featuring the bright flavors of lemon and cucumber.

Prep Time: 15 minutes

Ingredients:

- ✓ 2 cucumbers, peeled and chopped
- ✓ Zest and juice of 2 lemons
- ✓ 1 small red onion, chopped
- ✓ 2 cloves garlic, minced
- ✓ 3 cups vegetable broth
- ✓ 2 tablespoons extra-virgin olive oil
- ✓ Salt and black pepper to taste
- ✓ Lemon zest and fresh dill for garnish

Method:

1. Combine the chopped cucumbers, lemon zest, lemon juice, red onion, minced garlic, vegetable broth, and extra-virgin olive oil in a blender or food processor. Blend until smooth.
2. Season the Lemon Cucumber Gazpacho with salt and black pepper to taste. Adjust the seasoning if needed.
3. Chill the gazpacho in the refrigerator for at least 30 minutes before serving.
4. Serve the gazpacho cold, garnished with lemon zest and fresh dill.

Pineapple Coconut Gazpacho:

Pineapple Coconut Gazpacho is a tropical and creamy variation of gazpacho featuring the sweetness of pineapple and the richness of coconut milk.

Prep Time: 15 minutes

Ingredients:

- ✓ 2 cups fresh pineapple chunks
- ✓ 1 cucumber, peeled and chopped
- ✓ 1 small red onion, chopped
- ✓ 2 cloves garlic, minced
- ✓ 1 can (13.5 oz) coconut milk
- ✓ 3 cups vegetable broth
- ✓ 2 tablespoons lime juice
- ✓ Salt and black pepper to taste
- ✓ Fresh pineapple chunks and coconut flakes for garnish

Method:

1. Combine the fresh pineapple chunks, chopped cucumber, red onion, minced garlic, coconut milk, vegetable broth, and lime juice in a blender or food processor. Blend until smooth.
2. Season the Pineapple Coconut Gazpacho with salt and black pepper to taste. Adjust the seasoning if needed.
3. Chill the gazpacho in the refrigerator for at least 30 minutes before serving.
4. Serve the gazpacho cold, garnished with fresh pineapple chunks and coconut flakes.

Watercress and Almond Gazpacho:

Watercress and Almond Gazpacho is a vibrant green gazpacho featuring the peppery flavor of watercress and the nuttiness of almonds.

Prep Time: 15 minutes

Ingredients:

- ✓ 2 cups fresh watercress leaves
- ✓ 1/2 cup blanched almonds
- ✓ 1 cucumber, peeled and chopped
- ✓ 1 small red onion, chopped
- ✓ 2 cloves garlic, minced
- ✓ 3 cups vegetable broth
- ✓ 2 tablespoons sherry vinegar
- ✓ 2 tablespoons extra-virgin olive oil
- ✓ Salt and black pepper to taste
- ✓ Watercress leaves and toasted almond slices for garnish

Method:

1. Combine the fresh watercress leaves, blanched almonds, chopped cucumber, red onion, minced garlic, vegetable broth, sherry vinegar, and extra-virgin olive oil in a blender or food processor. Blend until smooth.
2. Season the Watercress and Almond Gazpacho with salt and black pepper to taste. Adjust the seasoning if needed.
3. Chill the gazpacho in the refrigerator for at least 30 minutes before serving.

4. Serve the gazpacho cold, garnished with watercress leaves and toasted almond slices.

Avocado Lime Gazpacho:

Avocado Lime Gazpacho is a creamy and tangy variation of gazpacho, featuring the richness of avocado and the zesty kick of lime.

Prep Time: 15 minutes

Ingredients:

- ✓ 2 ripe avocados, peeled and pitted
- ✓ Zest and juice of 2 limes
- ✓ 1 cucumber, peeled and chopped
- ✓ 1 small red onion, chopped
- ✓ 2 cloves garlic, minced
- ✓ 3 cups vegetable broth
- ✓ 2 tablespoons cilantro, chopped
- ✓ Salt and black pepper to taste
- ✓ Sliced avocado and lime wedges for garnish

Method:

1. Combine the ripe avocados, zest, lime juice, chopped cucumber, red onion, minced garlic, vegetable broth, and cilantro in a blender or food processor. Blend until smooth.
2. Season the Avocado Lime Gazpacho with salt and black pepper to taste. Adjust the seasoning if needed.
3. Chill the gazpacho in the refrigerator for at least 30 minutes before serving.
4. Serve the gazpacho cold, garnished with sliced avocado and lime wedges.

Roasted Eggplant Gazpacho:

Roasted Eggplant Gazpacho is a smoky and savory variation featuring the deep flavors of roasted eggplant.

Prep Time: 20 minutes

Ingredients:

- ✓ 2 medium eggplants, roasted, peeled, and chopped
- ✓ 1 cucumber, peeled and chopped
- ✓ 1 red bell pepper, roasted, peeled, and chopped
- ✓ 1 small red onion, chopped
- ✓ 2 cloves garlic, minced
- ✓ 3 cups vegetable broth
- ✓ 2 tablespoons red wine vinegar
- ✓ 2 tablespoons extra-virgin olive oil
- ✓ Salt and black pepper to taste
- ✓ Fresh basil leaves and croutons for garnish

Method:

1. Begin by roasting the eggplants and red bell pepper. Place them on a baking sheet and roast in the oven until the skins are charred, and the flesh is tender. Remove from the oven, let cool, then peel and chop.
2. Combine the roasted and chopped eggplant, red bell pepper, chopped cucumber, red onion, minced garlic, vegetable broth, red wine vinegar, and extra-virgin olive oil in a blender or food processor. Blend until smooth.
3. Season the Roasted Eggplant Gazpacho with salt and black pepper to taste. Adjust the seasoning if needed.

4. Chill the gazpacho in the refrigerator for at least 30 minutes before serving.
5. Serve the gazpacho cold, garnished with fresh basil leaves and croutons.

Thai Curry Gazpacho:

Thai Curry Gazpacho is a spicy and exotic twist on gazpacho, incorporating the flavors of Thai red curry paste and coconut milk.

> Prep Time: 15 minutes

Ingredients:

- ✓ 2 tablespoons Thai red curry paste (adjust to taste)
- ✓ 2 cans (13.5 oz each) coconut milk
- ✓ 1 cucumber, peeled and chopped
- ✓ 1 small red onion, chopped
- ✓ 2 cloves garlic, minced
- ✓ 3 cups vegetable broth
- ✓ 2 tablespoons lime juice
- ✓ Salt and black pepper to taste
- ✓ Fresh cilantro and sliced red chili for garnish

Method:

1. Heat the Thai red curry paste over medium heat in a large pot for a couple of minutes until fragrant.
2. Add the coconut milk, chopped cucumber, red onion, minced garlic, vegetable broth, and lime juice to the pot.

Stir well and bring to a simmer. Cook for about 5 minutes, allowing the flavors to meld.

3. Season the Thai Curry Gazpacho with salt and black pepper to taste. Adjust the seasoning if needed.
4. Chill the gazpacho in the refrigerator for at least 30 minutes before serving.
5. Serve the gazpacho cold, garnished with fresh cilantro and sliced red chili.

Kiwi Kiwifruit Gazpacho:

Kiwi Kiwifruit Gazpacho is a refreshing and tangy variation of gazpacho featuring the unique flavor of kiwifruit.

Prep Time: 15 minutes

Ingredients:

- ✓ 4 ripe kiwifruits, peeled and chopped
- ✓ 1 cucumber, peeled and chopped
- ✓ 1 small red onion, chopped
- ✓ 2 cloves garlic, minced
- ✓ 3 cups vegetable broth
- ✓ 2 tablespoons lime juice
- ✓ 2 tablespoons honey (or maple syrup for a vegan option)
- ✓ Salt and black pepper to taste
- ✓ Sliced kiwifruit and mint leaves for garnish

Method:

1. Combine the chopped kiwifruits, cucumber, red onion, minced garlic, vegetable broth, lime juice, and honey in a blender or food processor. Blend until smooth.
2. Season the Kiwi Kiwifruit Gazpacho with salt and black pepper to taste. Adjust the seasoning if needed.
3. Chill the gazpacho in the refrigerator for at least 30 minutes before serving.
4. Serve the gazpacho cold, garnished with sliced kiwifruit and mint leaves.

Tomato Basil Pesto Gazpacho:

Tomato Basil Pesto Gazpacho is a classic tomato-based gazpacho with the added depth of flavor from homemade basil pesto.

Prep Time: 15 minutes

Ingredients:

- ✓ 6 ripe tomatoes, chopped
- ✓ 1 cucumber, peeled and chopped
- ✓ 1 small red onion, chopped
- ✓ 2 cloves garlic, minced
- ✓ 3 cups vegetable broth
- ✓ 2 tablespoons red wine vinegar
- ✓ 2 tablespoons extra-virgin olive oil
- ✓ Salt and black pepper to taste
- ✓ Fresh basil leaves and homemade basil pesto for garnish

Method:

1. Combine the chopped tomatoes, cucumber, red onion, minced garlic, vegetable broth, red wine vinegar, and extra-virgin olive oil in a blender or food processor. Blend until smooth.
2. Season the Tomato Basil Pesto Gazpacho with salt and black pepper to taste. Adjust the seasoning if needed.
3. Chill the gazpacho in the refrigerator for at least 30 minutes before serving.
4. Serve the gazpacho cold, garnished with fresh basil leaves and a dollop of homemade basil pesto.

Smoked Salmon Gazpacho:

Smoked Salmon Gazpacho is a luxurious and savory variation of gazpacho featuring the rich flavors of smoked salmon and fresh vegetables.

Prep Time: 20 minutes

Ingredients:

- ✓ 4 oz smoked salmon, chopped
- ✓ 1 cucumber, peeled and chopped
- ✓ 1 small red onion, chopped
- ✓ 2 cloves garlic, minced
- ✓ 3 cups vegetable broth
- ✓ 2 tablespoons lemon juice
- ✓ 2 tablespoons fresh dill, chopped
- ✓ Salt and black pepper to taste
- ✓ Smoked salmon slices and dill sprigs for garnish

Method:

1. Combine the chopped smoked salmon, chopped cucumber, red onion, minced garlic, vegetable broth, lemon juice, and fresh dill in a blender or food processor. Blend until smooth.
2. Season the Smoked Salmon Gazpacho with salt and black pepper to taste. Adjust the seasoning if needed.
3. Chill the gazpacho in the refrigerator for at least 30 minutes before serving.
4. Serve the gazpacho cold, garnished with smoked salmon slices and dill sprigs.

Orange Cranberry Gazpacho:

Orange Cranberry Gazpacho is a sweet and tangy variation featuring the refreshing flavors of oranges and cranberries.

Prep Time: 15 minutes

Ingredients:

- ✓ 2 oranges, peeled and segmented
- ✓ 1 cup fresh cranberries
- ✓ 1 cucumber, peeled and chopped
- ✓ 1 small red onion, chopped
- ✓ 2 cloves garlic, minced
- ✓ 3 cups vegetable broth
- ✓ 2 tablespoons orange juice
- ✓ 2 tablespoons honey (or maple syrup for a vegan option)
- ✓ Salt and black pepper to taste
- ✓ Orange segments and fresh cranberries for garnish

Method:

1. Combine the peeled and segmented oranges, fresh cranberries, chopped cucumber, red onion, minced garlic, vegetable broth, orange juice, and honey in a blender or food processor. Blend until smooth.
2. Season the Orange Cranberry Gazpacho with salt and black pepper to taste. Adjust the seasoning if needed.
3. Chill the gazpacho in the refrigerator for at least 30 minutes before serving.
4. Serve the gazpacho cold, garnished with orange segments and fresh cranberries.

Blackberry Sage Gazpacho:

Blackberry Sage Gazpacho is a unique and fruity variation of gazpacho featuring the sweet-tart flavors of blackberries and aromatic sage.

Prep Time: 15 minutes

Ingredients:

- ✓ 2 cups fresh blackberries
- ✓ 1 cucumber, peeled and chopped
- ✓ 1 small red onion, chopped
- ✓ 2 cloves garlic, minced
- ✓ 3 cups vegetable broth
- ✓ 2 tablespoons red wine vinegar
- ✓ 2 tablespoons fresh sage leaves, chopped
- ✓ Salt and black pepper to taste
- ✓ Fresh blackberries and sage leaves for garnish

Method:

1. Combine the fresh blackberries, chopped cucumber, red onion, minced garlic, vegetable broth, red wine vinegar, and fresh sage leaves in a blender or food processor. Blend until smooth.
2. Season the Blackberry Sage Gazpacho with salt and black pepper to taste. Adjust the seasoning if needed.
3. Chill the gazpacho in the refrigerator for at least 30 minutes before serving.
4. Serve the gazpacho cold, garnished with fresh blackberries and sage leaves.

Plum Cinnamon Gazpacho:

Plum Cinnamon Gazpacho is a sweet and spiced variation of gazpacho featuring the rich flavors of plums and a hint of cinnamon.

Prep Time: 15 minutes

Ingredients:

- ✓ 2 cups ripe plums, pitted and chopped
- ✓ 1 cucumber, peeled and chopped
- ✓ 1 small red onion, chopped
- ✓ 2 cloves garlic, minced
- ✓ 3 cups vegetable broth
- ✓ 2 tablespoons balsamic vinegar
- ✓ 1/2 teaspoon ground cinnamon
- ✓ Salt and black pepper to taste
- ✓ Plum slices and cinnamon sticks for garnish

Method:

1. Combine the chopped ripe plums, cucumber, red onion, minced garlic, vegetable broth, balsamic vinegar, and ground cinnamon in a blender or food processor. Blend until smooth.
2. Season the Plum Cinnamon Gazpacho with salt and black pepper to taste. Adjust the seasoning if needed.
3. Chill the gazpacho in the refrigerator for at least 30 minutes before serving.
4. Serve the gazpacho cold, garnished with plum slices and cinnamon sticks.

Peach Habanero Gazpacho:

Peach Habanero Gazpacho is a spicy and fruity variation of gazpacho featuring peaches' sweetness and habanero peppers' heat.

Prep Time: 15 minutes

Ingredients:

- ✓ 2 ripe peaches, peeled and chopped
- ✓ 1 cucumber, peeled and chopped
- ✓ 1 small red onion, chopped
- ✓ 1 habanero pepper, seeds removed and minced (adjust to taste)
- ✓ 2 cloves garlic, minced
- ✓ 3 cups vegetable broth
- ✓ 2 tablespoons lime juice
- ✓ Salt and black pepper to taste
- ✓ Peach slices and habanero slices for garnish

Method:

1. In a blender or food processor, Combine the chopped ripe peaches, chopped cucumber, red onion, minced habanero pepper, minced garlic, vegetable broth, and lime juice. Blend until smooth.
2. Season the Peach Habanero Gazpacho with salt and black pepper to taste. Adjust the seasoning if needed.
3. Chill the gazpacho in the refrigerator for at least 30 minutes before serving.

4. Serve the gazpacho cold, garnished with peach and habanero slices.

Green Pea and Mint Gazpacho:

Green Pea and Mint Gazpacho is a vibrant and refreshing variation of gazpacho, featuring the sweetness of green peas and the coolness of mint.

Prep Time: 15 minutes

Ingredients:

- ✓ 2 cups fresh or frozen green peas, thawed
- ✓ 1 cucumber, peeled and chopped
- ✓ 1 small red onion, chopped
- ✓ 2 cloves garlic, minced
- ✓ 3 cups vegetable broth
- ✓ 2 tablespoons fresh mint leaves, chopped
- ✓ 2 tablespoons lemon juice
- ✓ Salt and black pepper to taste
- ✓ Fresh mint leaves and pea shoots for garnish

Method:

1. Combine the green peas, chopped cucumber, red onion, minced garlic, vegetable broth, fresh mint leaves, and lemon juice in a blender or food processor. Blend until smooth.
2. Season the Green Pea and Mint Gazpacho with salt and black pepper to taste. Adjust the seasoning if needed.
3. Chill the gazpacho in the refrigerator for at least 30 minutes before serving.
4. Serve the gazpacho cold, garnished with fresh mint leaves and pea shoots.

Radish Cilantro Gazpacho:

Radish Cilantro Gazpacho is a zesty and peppery variation of gazpacho, featuring the crispness of radishes and the bright flavor of cilantro.

Prep Time: 15 minutes

Ingredients:

- ✓ 2 cups radishes, chopped
- ✓ 1 cucumber, peeled and chopped
- ✓ 1 small red onion, chopped
- ✓ 2 cloves garlic, minced
- ✓ 3 cups vegetable broth
- ✓ 2 tablespoons fresh cilantro leaves, chopped
- ✓ 2 tablespoons lime juice
- ✓ Salt and black pepper to taste
- ✓ Sliced radishes and cilantro leaves for garnish

Method:

1. Combine the chopped radishes, chopped cucumber, red onion, minced garlic, vegetable broth, fresh cilantro leaves, and lime juice in a blender or food processor. Blend until smooth.
2. Season the Radish Cilantro Gazpacho with salt and black pepper to taste. Adjust the seasoning if needed.
3. Chill the gazpacho in the refrigerator for at least 30 minutes before serving.
4. Serve the gazpacho cold, garnished with sliced radishes and cilantro leaves.

Pine Nut and Rosemary Gazpacho:

Pine Nut and Rosemary Gazpacho is a rich and nutty variation featuring the earthy flavors of pine nuts and aromatic rosemary.

Prep Time: 15 minutes

Ingredients:

- ✓ 1/2 cup pine nuts
- ✓ 1 cucumber, peeled and chopped
- ✓ 1 small red onion, chopped
- ✓ 2 cloves garlic, minced
- ✓ 3 cups vegetable broth
- ✓ 2 tablespoons fresh rosemary leaves, chopped
- ✓ 2 tablespoons red wine vinegar
- ✓ Salt and black pepper to taste
- ✓ Toasted pine nuts and fresh rosemary sprigs for garnish

Method:

1. In a dry skillet, toast the pine nuts over medium heat until they are lightly golden and fragrant. Remove from the heat and let them cool.
2. Combine the toasted pine nuts, chopped cucumber, red onion, minced garlic, vegetable broth, fresh rosemary leaves, and vinegar in a blender or food processor. Blend until smooth.
3. Season the Pine Nut and Rosemary Gazpacho with salt and black pepper to taste. Adjust the seasoning if needed.

4. Chill the gazpacho in the refrigerator for at least 30 minutes before serving.
5. Serve the gazpacho cold, garnished with toasted pine nuts and fresh rosemary sprigs.

Cantaloupe Basil Gazpacho:

Cantaloupe Basil Gazpacho is a sweet and aromatic variation of gazpacho, featuring the luscious flavors of cantaloupe and fragrant basil.

Prep Time: 15 minutes

Ingredients:

- ✓ 2 cups ripe cantaloupe, peeled and chopped
- ✓ 1 cucumber, peeled and chopped
- ✓ 1 small red onion, chopped
- ✓ 2 cloves garlic, minced
- ✓ 3 cups vegetable broth
- ✓ 2 tablespoons fresh basil leaves, chopped
- ✓ 2 tablespoons balsamic vinegar
- ✓ Salt and black pepper to taste
- ✓ Cantaloupe balls and fresh basil leaves for garnish

Method:

1. Combine the chopped ripe cantaloupe, cucumber, red onion, minced garlic, vegetable broth, fresh basil leaves, and balsamic vinegar in a blender or food processor. Blend until smooth.
2. Season the Cantaloupe Basil Gazpacho with salt and black pepper to taste. Adjust the seasoning if needed.
3. Chill the gazpacho in the refrigerator for at least 30 minutes before serving.
4. Serve the gazpacho cold, garnished with cantaloupe balls and fresh basil leaves.

Artichoke Lemon Gazpacho:

Artichoke Lemon Gazpacho is a tangy and savory variation of gazpacho featuring the tartness of artichoke hearts and the brightness of lemon.

Prep Time: 15 minutes

Ingredients:

- ✓ 1 can (14 oz) artichoke hearts, drained and chopped
- ✓ 1 cucumber, peeled and chopped
- ✓ 1 small red onion, chopped
- ✓ 2 cloves garlic, minced
- ✓ 3 cups vegetable broth
- ✓ Zest and juice of 2 lemons
- ✓ 2 tablespoons fresh parsley, chopped
- ✓ Salt and black pepper to taste
- ✓ Lemon zest and parsley leaves for garnish

Method:

1. Combine the chopped artichoke hearts, cucumber, red onion, minced garlic, vegetable broth, lemon zest, and lemon juice in a blender or food processor. Blend until smooth.
2. Season the Artichoke Lemon Gazpacho with salt and black pepper to taste. Adjust the seasoning if needed.
3. Chill the gazpacho in the refrigerator for at least 30 minutes before serving.
4. Serve the gazpacho cold, garnished with lemon zest and parsley leaves.

Tamarind Tofu Gazpacho:

Tamarind Tofu Gazpacho is a tangy and protein-rich variation of gazpacho, featuring tamarind's unique flavor and tofu's creaminess.

Prep Time: 15 minutes

Ingredients:

- ✓ 1/4 cup tamarind paste
- ✓ 8 oz silken tofu
- ✓ 1 cucumber, peeled and chopped
- ✓ 1 small red onion, chopped
- ✓ 2 cloves garlic, minced
- ✓ 3 cups vegetable broth
- ✓ 2 tablespoons fresh cilantro, chopped
- ✓ Salt and black pepper to taste
- ✓ Tofu cubes and cilantro leaves for garnish

Method:

1. In a small bowl, dissolve the tamarind paste in a couple of tablespoons of warm water to create a tamarind concentrate.
2. Combine the tamarind concentrate, silken tofu, chopped cucumber, red onion, minced garlic, vegetable broth, and fresh cilantro in a blender or food processor. Blend until smooth.
3. Season the Tamarind Tofu Gazpacho with salt and black pepper to taste. Adjust the seasoning if needed.

4. Chill the gazpacho in the refrigerator for at least 30 minutes before serving.
5. Serve the gazpacho cold, garnished with tofu cubes and cilantro leaves.

Roasted Garlic Gazpacho:

Roasted Garlic Gazpacho is a rich and savory variation featuring the deep flavors of roasted garlic.

Prep Time: 20 minutes

Ingredients:

- ✓ 1 head of garlic
- ✓ 1 cucumber, peeled and chopped
- ✓ 1 small red onion, chopped
- ✓ 2 cloves garlic, minced
- ✓ 3 cups vegetable broth
- ✓ 2 tablespoons fresh basil, chopped
- ✓ 2 tablespoons red wine vinegar
- ✓ Salt and black pepper to taste
- ✓ Roasted garlic cloves and fresh basil leaves for garnish

Method:

1. Preheat the oven to 375°F (190°C). Slice off the top of the garlic head to expose the cloves. Drizzle with olive oil, wrap in foil, and roast for 30 minutes until the cloves are soft and golden. Let it cool.
2. Squeeze the roasted garlic cloves out of their skins and set them aside.
3. Combine the roasted garlic cloves, chopped cucumber, red onion, minced garlic, vegetable broth, fresh basil, and vinegar in a blender or food processor. Blend until smooth.

4. Season the Roasted Garlic Gazpacho with salt and black pepper to taste. Adjust the seasoning if needed.
5. Chill the gazpacho in the refrigerator for at least 30 minutes before serving.
6. Serve the gazpacho cold, garnished with roasted garlic cloves and fresh basil leaves.

Curry Cauliflower Gazpacho:

Curry Cauliflower Gazpacho is a spicy and creamy variation featuring curry spices' warmth and roasted cauliflower's richness.

Prep Time: 20 minutes

Ingredients:

- ✓ 1 small head of cauliflower, cut into florets
- ✓ 1 cucumber, peeled and chopped
- ✓ 1 small red onion, chopped
- ✓ 2 cloves garlic, minced
- ✓ 3 cups vegetable broth
- ✓ 2 tablespoons curry powder
- ✓ 2 tablespoons coconut milk
- ✓ Salt and black pepper to taste
- ✓ Fresh cilantro and coconut flakes for garnish

Method:

1. Preheat the oven to 400°F (200°C). Toss the cauliflower florets with olive oil and roast in the oven until tender and lightly browned, about 20-25 minutes. Let them cool.
2. Combine the roasted cauliflower florets, chopped cucumber, red onion, minced garlic, vegetable broth, curry powder, and coconut milk in a blender or food processor. Blend until smooth.
3. Season the Curry Cauliflower Gazpacho with salt and black pepper to taste. Adjust the seasoning if needed.

4. Chill the gazpacho in the refrigerator for at least 30 minutes before serving.
5. Serve the gazpacho cold, garnished with fresh cilantro and coconut flakes.

Apple Cider Vinegar Gazpacho:

Apple Cider Vinegar Gazpacho is a tangy and refreshing variation of gazpacho, featuring apple cider vinegar's bright acidity.

Prep Time: 15 minutes

Ingredients:

- ✓ 1/4 cup apple cider vinegar
- ✓ 1 cucumber, peeled and chopped
- ✓ 1 small red onion, chopped
- ✓ 2 cloves garlic, minced
- ✓ 3 cups vegetable broth
- ✓ 2 tablespoons fresh chives, chopped
- ✓ Salt and black pepper to taste
- ✓ Apple slices and chive sprigs for garnish

Method:

1. In a small bowl, Combine the apple cider vinegar with a couple of tablespoons of water.
2. Combine the diluted apple cider vinegar, chopped cucumber, red onion, minced garlic, vegetable broth, and fresh chives in a blender or food processor. Blend until smooth.
3. Season the Apple Cider Vinegar Gazpacho with salt and black pepper to taste. Adjust the seasoning if needed.
4. Chill the gazpacho in the refrigerator for at least 30 minutes before serving.

5. Serve the gazpacho cold, garnished with apple slices and chive sprigs.

Cranberry Orange Gazpacho:

Cranberry Orange Gazpacho is a sweet and tangy variation of gazpacho featuring the vibrant flavors of cranberries and oranges.

Prep Time: 15 minutes

Ingredients:

- ✓ 1 cup fresh cranberries
- ✓ Zest and juice of 2 oranges
- ✓ 1 cucumber, peeled and chopped
- ✓ 1 small red onion, chopped
- ✓ 2 cloves garlic, minced
- ✓ 3 cups vegetable broth
- ✓ 2 tablespoons honey (or maple syrup for a vegan option)
- ✓ Salt and black pepper to taste
- ✓ Fresh cranberries and orange zest for garnish

Method:

1. Combine the fresh cranberries, orange zest, orange juice, chopped cucumber, red onion, minced garlic, vegetable broth, and honey in a blender or food processor. Blend until smooth.
2. Season the Cranberry Orange Gazpacho with salt and black pepper to taste. Adjust the seasoning if needed.
3. Chill the gazpacho in the refrigerator for at least 30 minutes before serving.
4. Serve the gazpacho cold, garnished with fresh cranberries and orange zest.

Date and Almond Gazpacho:

Date and Almond Gazpacho is a sweet and nutty variation of gazpacho featuring dates' natural sweetness and almonds' richness.

> Prep Time: 15 minutes

Ingredients:

- ✓ 1/2 cup pitted dates, soaked in warm water for 10 minutes and drained
- ✓ 1/2 cup almonds, soaked in warm water for 10 minutes and drained
- ✓ 1 cucumber, peeled and chopped
- ✓ 1 small red onion, chopped
- ✓ 2 cloves garlic, minced
- ✓ 3 cups vegetable broth
- ✓ 2 tablespoons fresh parsley, chopped
- ✓ Salt and black pepper to taste
- ✓ Sliced almonds and chopped dates for garnish

Method:

1. Combine the soaked dates, almonds, chopped cucumber, red onion, minced garlic, vegetable broth, and fresh parsley in a blender or food processor. Blend until smooth.
2. Season the Date and Almond Gazpacho with salt and black pepper to taste. Adjust the seasoning if needed.
3. Chill the gazpacho in the refrigerator for at least 30 minutes before serving.

4. Serve the gazpacho cold, garnished with sliced almonds and chopped dates.

Pomegranate Walnut Gazpacho:

Pomegranate Walnut Gazpacho is a sweet and nutty variation of gazpacho, featuring the vibrant flavors of pomegranate and the richness of walnuts.

Prep Time: 15 minutes

Ingredients:

- ✓ 1/2 cup pomegranate seeds
- ✓ 1/2 cup walnuts
- ✓ 1 cucumber, peeled and chopped
- ✓ 1 small red onion, chopped
- ✓ 2 cloves garlic, minced
- ✓ 3 cups vegetable broth
- ✓ 2 tablespoons fresh mint leaves, chopped
- ✓ Salt and black pepper to taste
- ✓ Pomegranate seeds and chopped walnuts for garnish

Method:

1. Combine the pomegranate seeds, walnuts, chopped cucumber, red onion, minced garlic, vegetable broth, and fresh mint leaves in a blender or food processor. Blend until smooth.
2. Season the Pomegranate Walnut Gazpacho with salt and black pepper to taste. Adjust the seasoning if needed.
3. Chill the gazpacho in the refrigerator for at least 30 minutes before serving.
4. Serve the gazpacho cold, garnished with pomegranate seeds and chopped walnuts.

Black Bean and Corn Gazpacho:

Black Bean and Corn Gazpacho is a hearty and flavorful variation featuring a combination of black beans and sweet corn.

Prep Time: 15 minutes

Ingredients:

- ✓ 1 can (15 oz) black beans, drained and rinsed
- ✓ 1 cup corn kernels (fresh or frozen)
- ✓ 1 cucumber, peeled and chopped
- ✓ 1 small red onion, chopped
- ✓ 2 cloves garlic, minced
- ✓ 3 cups vegetable broth
- ✓ 2 tablespoons fresh cilantro, chopped
- ✓ 2 tablespoons lime juice
- ✓ Salt and black pepper to taste
- ✓ Sliced avocado and cilantro leaves for garnish

Method:

1. Combine the black beans, corn kernels, chopped cucumber, red onion, minced garlic, vegetable broth, fresh cilantro, and lime juice in a blender or food processor. Blend until smooth.
2. Season the Black Bean and Corn Gazpacho with salt and black pepper to taste. Adjust the seasoning if needed.
3. Chill the gazpacho in the refrigerator for at least 30 minutes before serving.

4. Serve the gazpacho cold, garnished with sliced avocado and cilantro leaves.

Rhubarb Strawberry Gazpacho:

Rhubarb Strawberry Gazpacho is a sweet and tart variation of gazpacho featuring the unique flavors of rhubarb and strawberries.

Prep Time: 15 minutes

Ingredients:

- ✓ 1 cup rhubarb, chopped
- ✓ 1 cup strawberries, hulled and chopped
- ✓ 1 cucumber, peeled and chopped
- ✓ 1 small red onion, chopped
- ✓ 2 cloves garlic, minced
- ✓ 3 cups vegetable broth
- ✓ 2 tablespoons fresh mint leaves, chopped
- ✓ Salt and black pepper to taste
- ✓ Sliced strawberries and mint leaves for garnish

Method:

1. Combine the chopped rhubarb and strawberries in a saucepan with a little water. Simmer over low heat until the rhubarb is tender, about 5-7 minutes. Let it cool.
2. Combine the cooked rhubarb, strawberries, chopped cucumber, red onion, minced garlic, vegetable broth, and fresh mint leaves in a blender or food processor. Blend until smooth.
3. Season the Rhubarb Strawberry Gazpacho with salt and black pepper to taste. Adjust the seasoning if needed.

4. Chill the gazpacho in the refrigerator for at least 30 minutes before serving.
5. Serve the gazpacho cold, garnished with sliced strawberries and mint leaves.

Asparagus Spinach Gazpacho:

Asparagus Spinach Gazpacho is a vibrant and green variation of gazpacho, featuring asparagus and spinach's freshness.

Prep Time: 15 minutes

Ingredients:

- ✓ 1 bunch of asparagus, tough ends trimmed and chopped
- ✓ 1 cup fresh spinach leaves
- ✓ 1 cucumber, peeled and chopped
- ✓ 1 small red onion, chopped
- ✓ 2 cloves garlic, minced
- ✓ 3 cups vegetable broth
- ✓ 2 tablespoons fresh basil leaves, chopped
- ✓ Salt and black pepper to taste
- ✓ Asparagus tips and basil leaves for garnish

Method:

1. Blanch the asparagus tips for about 2 minutes in a pot of boiling water until they are bright green. Drain and set aside for garnish.
2. Combine the chopped asparagus (excluding the tips), fresh spinach leaves, chopped cucumber, red onion, minced garlic, vegetable broth, and fresh basil leaves in a blender or food processor. Blend until smooth.
3. Season the Asparagus Spinach Gazpacho with salt and black pepper to taste. Adjust the seasoning if needed.
4. Chill the gazpacho in the refrigerator for at least 30 minutes before serving.

5. Serve the gazpacho cold, garnished with blanched asparagus tips and basil leaves.

Fig and Prosciutto Gazpacho:

Fig and Prosciutto Gazpacho is a sweet and savory variation of gazpacho, featuring the delightful combination of figs and prosciutto.

Prep Time: 15 minutes

Ingredients:

- ✓ 6 ripe figs, stemmed and chopped
- ✓ 3 slices of prosciutto, chopped
- ✓ 1 cucumber, peeled and chopped
- ✓ 1 small red onion, chopped
- ✓ 2 cloves garlic, minced
- ✓ 3 cups vegetable broth
- ✓ 2 tablespoons fresh thyme leaves, chopped
- ✓ Salt and black pepper to taste
- ✓ Prosciutto strips and fresh thyme sprigs for garnish

Method:

1. Combine the chopped figs, prosciutto, cucumber, red onion, minced garlic, vegetable broth, and fresh thyme leaves in a blender or food processor. Blend until smooth.
2. Season the Fig and Prosciutto Gazpacho with salt and black pepper to taste. Adjust the seasoning if needed.
3. Chill the gazpacho in the refrigerator for at least 30 minutes before serving.
4. Serve the gazpacho cold, garnished with prosciutto strips and fresh thyme sprigs.

Grapefruit Jalapeño Gazpacho:

Grapefruit Jalapeño Gazpacho is a zesty and spicy variation of gazpacho, featuring grapefruit's bright flavors and the jalapeño peppers' heat.

Prep Time: 15 minutes

Ingredients:

- ✓ 2 grapefruits, peeled and segmented
- ✓ 1 cucumber, peeled and chopped
- ✓ 1 small red onion, chopped
- ✓ 1 jalapeño pepper, seeds removed and minced (adjust to taste)
- ✓ 2 cloves garlic, minced
- ✓ 3 cups vegetable broth
- ✓ 2 tablespoons fresh cilantro, chopped
- ✓ Salt and black pepper to taste
- ✓ Grapefruit segments and cilantro leaves for garnish

Method:

1. Combine the grapefruit segments, chopped cucumber, red onion, minced jalapeño pepper, garlic, vegetable broth, and fresh cilantro in a blender or food processor. Blend until smooth.
2. Season the Grapefruit Jalapeño Gazpacho with salt and black pepper to taste. Adjust the seasoning if needed.
3. Chill the gazpacho in the refrigerator for at least 30 minutes before serving.

4. Serve the gazpacho cold, garnished with grapefruit segments and cilantro leaves.

Roasted Tomato Gazpacho with Shrimp:

Roasted Tomato Gazpacho with Shrimp is a hearty and satisfying variation featuring the smoky flavors of roasted tomatoes and succulent shrimp.

Prep Time: 30 minutes

Ingredients:

- ✓ 4 large tomatoes, halved
- ✓ 1 cucumber, peeled and chopped
- ✓ 1 small red onion, chopped
- ✓ 2 cloves garlic, minced
- ✓ 3 cups vegetable broth
- ✓ 2 tablespoons fresh basil, chopped
- ✓ 8 large cooked shrimp, peeled and deveined
- ✓ Salt and black pepper to taste
- ✓ Fresh basil leaves for garnish

Method:

1. Preheat the oven to 400°F (200°C). Place the halved tomatoes on a baking sheet, cut side up, and roast them for about 20-25 minutes until they are soft and slightly charred. Let them cool.
2. Combine the roasted tomatoes, chopped cucumber, red onion, minced garlic, vegetable broth, and fresh basil in a blender or food processor. Blend until smooth.
3. Season the Roasted Tomato Gazpacho with salt and black pepper to taste. Adjust the seasoning if needed.

4. Chill the gazpacho in the refrigerator for at least 30 minutes before serving.
5. Serve the gazpacho cold, garnished with cooked shrimp and fresh basil leaves.

Pistachio Dill Gazpacho:

Pistachio Dill Gazpacho is a creamy and herby variation of gazpacho, featuring the richness of pistachios and the aromatic dill.

Prep Time: 15 minutes

Ingredients:

- ✓ 1/2 cup shelled pistachios
- ✓ 1 cucumber, peeled and chopped
- ✓ 1 small red onion, chopped
- ✓ 2 cloves garlic, minced
- ✓ 3 cups vegetable broth
- ✓ 2 tablespoons fresh dill, chopped
- ✓ Salt and black pepper to taste
- ✓ Pistachio nuts and dill fronds for garnish

Method:

1. Combine the shelled pistachios, chopped cucumber, red onion, minced garlic, vegetable broth, and fresh dill in a blender or food processor. Blend until smooth.
2. Season the Pistachio Dill Gazpacho with salt and black pepper to taste. Adjust the seasoning if needed.
3. Chill the gazpacho in the refrigerator for at least 30 minutes before serving.
4. Serve the gazpacho cold, garnished with pistachio nuts and dill fronds.

Miso Shiitake Gazpacho:

Miso Shiitake Gazpacho is a savory and umami-packed variation of gazpacho, featuring the depth of miso and the earthy shiitake mushrooms.

Prep Time: 20 minutes

Ingredients:

- ✓ 1 cup shiitake mushrooms, chopped
- ✓ 1 cucumber, peeled and chopped
- ✓ 1 small red onion, chopped
- ✓ 2 cloves garlic, minced
- ✓ 3 cups vegetable broth
- ✓ 2 tablespoons white miso paste
- ✓ Salt and black pepper to taste
- ✓ Sliced shiitake mushrooms and chopped green onions for garnish

Method:

1. In a skillet, sauté the chopped shiitake mushrooms over medium heat until tender and slightly browned. Let them cool.
2. Combine the sautéed shiitake mushrooms, chopped cucumber, red onion, minced garlic, vegetable broth, and white miso paste in a blender or food processor. Blend until smooth.
3. Season the Miso Shiitake Gazpacho with salt and black pepper to taste. Adjust the seasoning if needed.

4. Chill the gazpacho in the refrigerator for at least 30 minutes before serving.
5. Serve the gazpacho cold, garnished with sliced shiitake mushrooms and chopped green onions.

Printed in Great Britain
by Amazon

42234452R10046